T0065602

Kene D. Ewulu, Ed.D.

CHRIST-LED REBOUND SERIES

DEPRESSION, OPPRESSION, AND POSSESSION

WESTBOW
P R E S S®
A DIVISION OF THOMAS NELSON
& ZONDERVAN

Scripture taken from the King James Version of the Bible.

Scripture taken from the Holy Bible, NEW INTERNATIONAL VERSION®. Copyright © 1973, 1978, 1984, 2011 by Biblica, Inc. All rights reserved worldwide. Used by permission. NEW INTERNATIONAL VERSION® and NIV® are registered trademarks of Biblica, Inc. Use of either trademark for the offering of goods or services requires the prior written consent of Biblica US, Inc.

Revised Standard Version of the Bible, copyright ©1952 [2nd edition, 1971] by the Division of Christian Education of the National Council of the Churches of Christ in the United States of America. Used by permission. All rights reserved.

This book is a work of non-fiction. Unless otherwise noted, the author and the publisher make no explicit guarantees as to the accuracy of the information contained in this book and in some cases, names of people and places have been altered to protect their privacy.

WestBow Press books may be ordered through booksellers or by contacting:

WestBow Press
A Division of Thomas Nelson & Zondervan
1663 Liberty Drive
Bloomington, IN 47403
www.westbowpress.com
1 (866) 928-1240

Because of the dynamic nature of the Internet, any web addresses or links contained in this book may have changed since publication and may no longer be valid. The views expressed in this work are solely those of the author and do not necessarily reflect the views of the publisher, and the publisher hereby disclaims any responsibility for them.

Any people depicted in stock imagery provided by Thinkstock are models, and such images are being used for illustrative purposes only. Certain stock imagery © Thinkstock.

ISBN: 978-1-5127-5319-6 (sc)
ISBN: 978-1-5127-5318-9 (e)

Library of Congress Control Number: 2016913215

Print information available on the last page.

WestBow Press rev. date: 08/12/2016

Contents

Author's Note vii

Dedication.. xiii

Preface xv

Defining Depression, Oppression, and Possession 1

Rebounding from Depression,

Oppression, and Possession 7

Victory through Jesus Christ.......................................27

Epilogue..31

Glossary 35

About the Author...43

Author's Note

In my first book titled *Christ-Led Rebound Principles: Sustaining Christian Deliverance and Victory,* which was published in 2013, I identified some of the issues that we struggle with in life. I also identified scripturally backed solutions and ways to keep our victory.

Many issues were addressed, but I realize that we all usually do not face more than one or two of them at a time. With the new series of books, I am addressing specific struggles that modern Christians and non-Christians face on a daily basis. These books will be available both in print and non-print media.

I am also highlighting action steps throughout the book. These are places where I encourage you to stop for a minute and reflect inward. You may want to see if anything you have read applies to you or your loved ones. You should end with a prayer as the Lord leads you.

> *Action Steps are between you and God. Please try to be as open and honest as you can.*

I have been led to break up the original book into small booklets that deal with these singular struggles or "yokes" and to delve deeper into the action steps we must embrace to be delivered from them and to live free, victorious lives in Christ. The first two parts of the *Christ-Led Rebound Series* dealt with "Inactivity" and "Bad Habits" respectively; they are already published, and paperback or e-book formats can be ordered or downloaded at www.ReboundSeries.com.

This publication is the third of the *Christ-Led Rebound Series* and addresses "Depression, Oppression, and Possession." For ease of reference, I will subsequently address these struggles with the acronym DOP. This third part in the series will define these afflictions, trace how they relate to each other, and show a roadmap for recovering from them and retaining our dominion over them.

I humbly ask that you prayerfully read this booklet, meditate on it, and practice what you learn. For those who struggle with depression, oppression, and possession (DOP), you will find that much patience and reliance on God's grace are required. You will also find that it is possible, through the grace and strengthening of our Lord Jesus Christ, to live victoriously free from these yokes and to enjoy the peace that springs forth as you relate frequently with the Holy Spirit of God!

The thief cometh not, but for to steal, and to kill, and to destroy: I am come that they might have life, and that they might have it more abundantly. (John 10:10 KJV)

The thief comes only to steal and kill and destroy; I have come that they may have life, and have it to the full. (John 10:10 NIV)

The thief comes only to steal and kill and destroy; I came that they may have life, and have it abundantly. (John 10:10 RSV)

Dedication

This is dedicated to Angela Godwin-
Ewulu, my sister in every way.
You have allowed yourself to be a conduit for
God's never-ceasing encouragement for His
children and a useful vessel in the fight against
depression, oppression, and possession.
May you never grow weary in well-doing!

Preface

A significant portion of our society suffers from depression! Statistics show that about 7 percent of adults in the United States had at least one episode of depression in any year (National Institutes of Health, n.d.). This number is higher for older adults and may be climbing. The suicide rate is also climbing. Suicide is too often the end of this condition, while millions live intolerably with it.

Circumstances within and outside our control have conspired to reduce our self-esteem, self-belief, and confidence in our abilities and our relationships. We have become downcast because we do not see how our situations can be reversed; psychoanalysts, medications, and motivational sessions have not been as successful as we had hoped. We are only coping with depression and not beating it.

One thing we need to understand is that depression has spiritual undertones and can be vanquished by embracing God and His Christ—Jesus. Depression is often the key that leads to an even more severe condition of oppression and spiritual possession. In some of these instances, nightmares, delusions, and subservience to the devil can occur.

The good news is that Jesus is the head of all spiritual beings (Eph. 1:20–21, Col. 2:10) and has already won all our depressive, oppressive, and possessive battles! All we need to do is submit to and embrace Jesus, and everything else will fall into place. But before we embark on this rebound journey through DOP, I want us to take a very important action step now:

> *Pray for the millions living with*
> *depression.*
> *Ask God to reach them!*
> *Please try to be as open and honest as*
> *you can.*

Having performed this selfless act of love, I enjoin you to come along with me as we rediscover how to hide under the shadow of Christ and permanently break the yokes of depression, oppression, and possession.

Jesus reigns! May He also reign in your life!

Defining Depression, Oppression, and Possession

Christians live under the protection or umbrella of God! He strongly warns us *not* to conform to the world, preferring instead to offer us a condition in which the perfect will of God is in control in our lives. God asks us to present ourselves to Him (Romans 12:1–3). If one is not a believer, or if one's faith is unsure, it may be more of a struggle to control one's feelings when things do not go according to plan. In other words, we may pretend that our feelings are irrelevant or can somehow be overcome by our self-will. This can become the start of the journey down the dangerous slippery slope of DOP (depression, oppression, and possession).

The DOP state is often preceded by feelings of self-denial of God's faithfulness. We can begin to doubt that God is still in charge of everything in the affairs of people.

As you well know, we are what we think. This means our mental and emotional doubts concerning God's sovereignty in all things can negatively influence our minds. Loss of hope can lead to denial, and denial is a defense mechanism that acts as a prelude to a repressed state of mind. *Merriam-Webster's Dictionary* defines repression simply as "the act of not allowing a memory, feeling or desire to be expressed."

Whether this "bottling up" is intentional or not, it allows us to function, albeit in a limited manner, as we go about our daily activities. However, the fact that we put away uncomfortable memories does not mean they do not exist; they fester away

> Prayerfully consider yourself. Are there unresolved emotions and memories?
> Begin to ask God to reveal these things to you. and to speak the solutions to you. Ask Him to send you help!

within us, and eventually they lead to a depressed state of mind.

Defining Depression

Anyone dealing with a depressed state of mind can be classified as suffering from depression.

Depression can be described as the state of feeling sad, dejected, and hopeless. It can be characterized by inactivity, difficulty in thinking or concentrating, or suicidal tendencies. As we go through this gamut of emotions and thought processes, we actually begin to think (in error, of course) that God does not know or care about our current difficulties. The belief that the highest power ever, the God of creation, does not know or care about what happens to us can be a heavy load. Continued exposure to this manner of thinking can be crushing to our minds and spirits—a state of mind that I identify as *oppression*.

Defining Oppression

Oppression happens when we come under the thumb of the devil and his agents. An oppressed person is one who lives under the authority of an unjust or brutal system or individual. Any part of our lives can be oppressed, but perhaps the most devastating is our minds.

When the devil oppresses us, we become fearful, subdued, pessimistic, morose, and spiritually and mentally burdened. We do not expect anything good to happen to us, or for us, preferring to stay delusional, irrational, and temperamental and to assign blame to others for our failures or inadequacies. We can sometimes suffer nightmares and spiritual attacks, and we might not know when something is real or just a figment of our imaginations.

As we refuse to acknowledge our own inadequacies, we spurn any type of help that might be forthcoming from friends, relatives, or mental health professionals. It is even sadder to say that sustained exposure to oppressive rule can lead to a person becoming a willing or unwilling instrument in the hands of the devil. This is a very dangerous spiritual state, and help should be sought urgently if we suspect that we or our loved ones are approaching this realm. I call this the state of *possession*!

Prayerfully consider if you or a loved one has been responsible for causing pain to another. Could anyone possibly hold you responsible for some hurt he or she feels?

Defining Possession

Simply speaking, possession happens when we become subservient to the devil, allowing him to control us and use us for his purposes. A subtle change in our personality occurs, and we cause others to stumble in their walks with God through our distractive and annoying actions.

I do not say here that we go about transfigured into something physically and socially ugly but that we somehow become harbingers of sadness, strife, and negativity, often playing the devil's advocate and engendering discontent whenever we are part of a gathering! It is like we borrow another personality that promises to elevate us again, regardless of the consequences to others.

It may be difficult to understand why people would want to live like this—hurting others, frustrating family and loved ones, and alienating friends. One of the reasons is that this condition can offer them some degree of power or control in their situations. Although negative (and they know it), they have been fooled into thinking that this is the only way they can strike back or protect themselves. Ministers and intercessors will often hear them confess, "I don't know why I do this." The pertinent question here is, are you experiencing depression, oppression, or possession?

Are you DOPed?

Rebounding from Depression, Oppression, and Possession

> For God so loved the world, that he gave his only begotten Son, that whosoever believeth in him should not perish, but have everlasting life. (John 3:16 KJV)

People who abuse drugs often use the term *doping*. I cannot help but draw on the similarities between the totally evanescent pleasure that drug addicts crave and this equally destructive mental state. Both of them take an innocent child of God and create a crushed victim who constantly faces failure and defeat. I call this the *doped condition*.

Those going through the doped condition are not often aware of their precariously dangerous situation, but as intercessors, we need to learn how to recognize the early warning signs. Utilizing the same enthusiasm and sense of urgency that you would use to steer your loved child away from a drug, we should also prayerfully address the early signs of a repressed, depressed individual. As everyone knows, it becomes more taxing further down the road to reverse the ravages of drug addiction—or of a doped condition.

Rebounding from depression, oppression, and possession can be achieved by internalizing certain age-old truths and practical steps. These truths are outlined below, but we will be categorizing them further. This helps us quickly identify where the solutions to our predicaments can be found.

Action Step

Pray for a sharp, teachable mind at this time.

We will now list these truths, examine categorized action steps and supporting scriptures, and identify how these biblical verses can work personally for us.

- **Think positively and accept God's mercy.**
  (Lamentations 3:22–23)

- **Only God can forgive completely.**
  (Psalm 103:11–13)

- **Study and contemplate the Bible.**
  (2 Timothy 2:15)

- **God still loves you and always will.**
  (Romans 8:38–39)

- **Accept prayer, advice, and medical attention.**
  (James 5:14–15)

- **Embrace and jealously guard God's joy within you.**
  (Psalm 28:7)

- **Ask for and believe in the healing power of Jesus's name.**
  (John 14:13–14)

- **Worship God in songs as frequently as you can.**
  (Psalm 95:1–8)

- **Believe that God will hear and fully deliver you.**
  (Psalm 107:19–20)

As we dwell briefly on these points, let us invite the Holy Spirit to come into our hearts and teach us all things.

By doing so, we will overcome our peculiar challenges and be victorious again. God's word is powerful and can break any hold of the enemy on our lives. We just have to believe God, trust Him, and step into our destiny; the end is sure!

Repression as a Precursor to DOP

Having identified repression as often being the beginning phase of depression, oppression, and possession (DOP), I want to touch a little bit on the three steps we can take to reject repressive feelings in our lives.

> ### Rejecting Repression
> - Avoid negative reports.
> - Remember God's promises.
> - Remember that God forgives.

- **Avoid negative reports, and embrace God's permanent mercy.**

The psalmist supports this by saying, "I will sing of the mercies of the Lord forever: with my mouth will I make known thy faithfulness to all generations" (Psalm 89:1 KJV).

Share with God, and others, about the mercy and grace you received in overcoming past difficulties. You bring other people to God when you talk of His faithfulness and renewal in your own life.

- **Constantly remind and reassure yourself of God's promises concerning you.**

We are reminded of God's intention to enrich us: "Beloved, I wish above all things that thou mayest prosper and be in health, even as thy soul prospereth" (3 John 2 KJV).

This is particularly important because it deals with the present and enables you to look forward with hope and expectation to God's imminent intervention and resolution of your current problems. Speak these words back to God in prayer; His words never lie, and they will accomplish everything they address. Your faith is also reinforced when you speak God's words back to Him.

> So then faith cometh by hearing, and hearing by the word of God. (Romans 10:17 KJV)

■ **Remember that it is God who decides to forgive; no explanations or permissions to do so are needed.**

Be reminded that God is the sovereign and ultimate ruler:

> For He saith to Moses, I will have mercy on whom I will have mercy, and I will have compassion on whom I will have compassion. So then it is not of him that willeth, nor of him that runneth, but of God that sheweth mercy. (Romans 9:15–16 KJV)

Mercy, grace, and forgiveness are gifts from God; no one can work for, or achieve them. Therefore, accept them graciously so that humility and newness can be established in your walk with God. Likewise, accord mercy, grace, and forgiveness to others in accordance with Jesus's charge: "Freely you have received, freely give" (Matthew 10:8 KJV).

These three reminders are based upon our diligence in searching God's Word for His promises. We are to think and stay positive, remember God's promises from the Bible, and recite them to ourselves when we feel the denial of God's faithfulness creeping into our minds.

We Must Read the Bible as Often as We Can!

The secret to overcoming challenges lies in studying and contemplating (thinking deeply) on the word of God.

Rebounding from Depression

I have identified four steps here, and even though I know there are many more, the steps outlined below cover the basics for overcoming depression.

Rebounding from Depression

- Meditate on pure thoughts
- Believe that God loves you
- Ask for help
- Actively seek out or cultivate joy

- *Meditate on pure thoughts and the promises of God by studying the Bible and internalizing God's promises concerning your circumstances.*

    This precept is addressed in the Bible in the following manner:

    And be not conformed to this world: but be ye transformed by the renewing of your mind, that ye may prove what is that good, and acceptable, and perfect, will of God. (Romans 12:2 KJV)

    Once again, emphasize studying God's word!

- *Believe that God still loves you, and always will.*

    We are reminded of the need to trust that God loves us and will soon come through on our behalf: "Rest in the Lord, and wait patiently for him" (Psalm 37:7a KJV).

Accept God's love and forgiveness, and do not allow the guilt of past mistakes to creep in. God completely washes our mistakes away when He forgives; as far as He is concerned, we never sinned. It does not make sense to remind our God of things He has chosen to forget—of things that, as far as He is concerned, did not happen!

- *Ask for spiritual intervention, prayers, or advice. Get medical attention where necessary.*

> The apostle James reiterates these points by commanding, "Is any sick among you? Let him call for the elders of the church; and let them pray over him, anointing him with oil in the name of the Lord: And the prayer of faith shall save the sick, and the Lord shall raise him up; and if he have committed sins, they shall be forgiven him" (James 5:14–15 KJV).

Don't be too shy to ask others to pray for you or to seek friendly and professional advice. In certain cases, get medical help. Divine healing can sometimes come through the ability of your body and mind to respond to medication or psychiatric advice. Go ahead and allow God to use whatever means He so desires to heal and transform you; He has so many at His disposal!

- *Open yourself up to God's joy. Do not let your divine joyfulness wane.*

    We are encouraged to be joyful because of its inherent medicinal effects: "A merry heart doeth good like a medicine: but a broken spirit drieth the bones" (Proverbs 17:22 KJV).

God tells us that His joy is the strength we need to overcome our difficulties. Therefore, if we can protect our joy, we have the necessary ingredient to stay strong in the face of the devil's attacks and to win. Recently, scientific studies have shown that individuals who are happy obtain benefits that include satisfaction, longevity, disease regression, and better relationships. But the world will agree that earthly happiness depends on circumstances and is fleeting. In order to stay happy, people have resorted to relentless activity, which is sometimes selfish, unsafe, and at times, distasteful. This is why God calls us higher to joy, which we can only find with Him.

Think therefore on the good things God has done and stay joyful, even in the midst of your challenges. He wants to be valued during our mountaintop experiences (victories), but more importantly, God wants us to seek and abide in Him during our valley experiences (trials, failures, and challenges)!

Rebounding from Oppression

As I said in the earlier part of this book where we defined terms, oppression often results from remaining depressed over a period of time. Therefore, if you or your loved ones find that you are being oppressed in your emotions or mind, you may also need to go back and review the steps to dealing with depression.

Rebounding From Oppression
- Deal with depression
- Prayer of deliverance
- Have faith in God
- Praise and Worship

- *Be open to deliverance by asking for prayers from Christian elders and brethren. Have faith in the healing power of the name of Jesus.*

Again, the biblical advice is to: "ask your spiritual leaders for prayers" (James 5:14 KJV).

> Jesus confirms the healing power of His disciples by saying, "And these signs shall follow them that believe; in my name shall they cast out devils; they shall speak with new tongues; they shall take up serpents; and if they drink any deadly thing, it shall not hurt them; they shall lay hands on the sick, and they shall recover" (Mark 16:17–18 KJV).

In essence, your trusted spiritual leaders (pastors, friends, and mentors) have been given the power to pray for you and supernaturally drive away any negative spirits that might have been tormenting you. Submit yourself to them and the Holy Spirit, share your challenges with them, and receive your healing as you agree with their prayers. Be strengthened in the knowledge that God is working through them for your benefit.

- *By faith, receive God's power that releases those who believe from the devil's bondage.*

> God's power is available for our healing: "And it shall come to pass in that day, that his burden shall be taken away from off thy shoulder, and his yoke from off thy neck, and the yoke shall be destroyed because of the anointing" (Isaiah 10:27 KJV).

This is the very reason why Bible-believing churches invite us to come forward for prayer during services, or have a prayer line, e-mail, or other media available. God honors His word by giving His shepherds authority to speak deliverance to the flock. We are being asked here to believe that God's delivering power has been released unto us through prayer of the elders and the laying on of hands. With faith in God's ability and willingness to save, everything the devil has thrown at us is repelled, and whatever we lost as a result of his attacks will be restored back to us manifold.

> This promise of restoration is confirmed in the book of Joel: "And I will restore to you the years that the locust hath eaten, the cankerworm, and

the caterpillar, and the palmerworm, my great army which I sent among you. And ye shall eat in plenty, and be satisfied, and praise the name of the Lord your God that hath dealt wondrously with you: and my people shall never be ashamed" (Joel 2:25–26 KJV).

There are instances where lasting or permanent effects of DOP exist, such as divorce or loss of employment. God is able to provide healing from past hurts, peace, joy, a new relationship, or a new job in these instances. One thing that is certain is that when God restores, He has the freedom to decide what He restores, what He replaces, or which new blessings He brings our way. We just have to trust that He will do so in His own perfect time!

- *Praise and worship God as frequently as possible.*

  The potency of worship and praise to God in the midst of difficult times is demonstrated in the story of Paul and Silas. As faithful followers of Jesus, who preached the gospel to the gentiles, they were imprisoned in a dungeon and their fate was desperate, if not hopeless. But as they lifted up their voices and sang praises to God in the night, the Bible tells us that their chains were loosened and the gates broke open: "And at midnight Paul and Silas prayed, and sang praises unto God: and the prisoners heard them. And suddenly there was a great earthquake, so that the foundations of the prison were shaken: and immediately all the doors were opened, and every one's bands were loosed" (Acts 15:25–26 KJV).

Praising and worshiping God, especially during our most difficult times, is sweet and wonderful music to His ears. It tells God that we are willing to follow Him unconditionally, regardless of our situation. Singing unto Him in the midst of our storms moves God's hands on our behalf in mighty ways, and people are drawn to Him as they witness our miraculous delivery from unpleasant circumstances. The account of King Jehoshaphat and the worship-led military victory of the heavily outnumbered Israelite army over the armies of Seir, Ammon, and Moab (2 Chron. 20:22) clearly testifies to God's intervention when worship is offered up to Him during stormy times.

Worship is the highest form of battle and happens when we praise God without any hindrances. We exalt Him because of who He is and not because of what we expect Him to do for us. We are to worship God as often as we can, listening to, and singing praise and worship songs. When this is done in faith, God's mighty hand will surely come upon our health, family, and finances.

Rebounding from Possession

For those who are so far gone that they are no longer in control of their actions, we call this spiritual possession, and only the Lord God can restore them. Just as with other elements of the "doped" condition, we need to review and address the action steps for depression and oppression first. We especially need help and prayers from spiritual elders.

> **Rebounding from Possession**
> - Repent and renounce the devil's grasp on your life.
> - Trust God for complete healing.

The Bible tells us that we cannot serve two masters at the same time. In order to work effectively for one employer, we have to sever our ties with other interests. This applies in politics, industry, and also in spiritual matters.

- *Repent and renounce the devil's grasp on your life*

> The Bible instructs that the first step to regaining all we lost to the devil is repentance and refusal to go back on the old, sinful road: "If my people, which are called by my name, shall humble themselves, and pray, and seek my face, and turn from their wicked ways; then will I hear from heaven, and will forgive their sin, and will heal their land" (2 Chronicles 7:14 KJV).

The first thing we need to realize is that our actions or inactions did not glorify God but only served God's enemy, the devil. We need at this time to denounce the devil, repent from our behaviors, and turn back to God. We must make every effort not to repeat the actions that got us into trouble in the first place! This is true repentance, and the Lord often gives strength for overcoming temptations when we ask Him.

> In the Bible (Luke 8), we learn of several of Jesus's disciples who were important in His ministry. Some of these had been tormented by

evil spirits until Jesus released them. We can be released too. Jesus declared that when He sets us free, we will be completely unfettered from everything that previously ailed us: "If the Son therefore shall make you free, you shall be free indeed" (John 8:36 KJV).

- *Ask the Lord in faith for your healing and deliverance; He will hear you and permanently deliver you from all your afflictions.*

    The Psalmist confirms this by saying, "Then they cry unto the Lord in their trouble, and He saveth them out of their distresses. He sent His Word, and healed them, and delivered them from their destructions" (Psalm 107:19–20 KJV).

    Regardless of how varied and severe our issues are, we are rest assured that the Creator of the universe is willing and able to get us through them all: "Many are the afflictions of the righteous: but the Lord delivereth him out of them all" (Psalm 34:19 KJV).

God has promised, and countless situations in the Bible attest that nothing is too difficult for God to change—nothing! He will deliver us because of our faith in Him, because of the actions we embrace on account of our newly renewed faith, and because good ultimately triumphs over evil.

The most wonderful thing about this entire situation is that not only will we be set free from the things that depress, oppress, or possess us (DOP), but ... *our freedom will also be irrevocable and permanent!*

Victory through Jesus Christ

Repressions, depressions, oppressions, and possessions happen! They occur as we navigate our lives from the domination of the devil to the love and freedom that exists in serving the Lord Jesus.

> The Bible (God's word) has a response for us as we go through these afflictions: "Come, and let us return unto the Lord: for He hath torn, and he will heal us; He hath smitten, and he will bind us up" (Hosea 6:1 KJV).

Even though we are currently besieged and it seems as if there is no hope, I urge us to trust that if we turn to God, He will heal us and bind up our wounds.

> He promised to do so: "We are troubled on every side, yet not distressed; we are perplexed, but not in despair; persecuted, but not forsaken;

cast down, but not destroyed" (2 Corinthians 4:8–9 KJV).

Jesus is calling us today to come as we are— as broken, hopeless, despondent, depressed, and oppressed as ever.

> He wants to help us, even as He promised: "Come unto me, all ye that labor and are heavy laden, and I will give you rest. Take my yoke upon you, and learn of me; for I am meek and lowly in heart: and ye shall find rest unto your souls. For my yoke is easy, and my burden is light" (Matthew 11:28–30 KJV).

As we go on, we will find that certain steps or tenets are always important. We cannot overcome or rebound without these habits.

I urge us to hold on … not to give up … to look to God and to keep reading the Bible, praying, worshiping, believing, trusting, patiently waiting, and thanking Him for our anticipated healing, restoration, and victorious new life.

If the challenging situation is just beginning, God can heal. When God heals, He will also restore all that was lost during the times of affliction. And if the situation is considered by others to be too far gone, God can resurrect and bring new life to that peculiar circumstance. *Our God is without any doubt the God of resurrection!*

May the loving Father who resurrected Jesus from the dead uphold you, and may He cause you to live a rich, fulfilling, and inspiring life. Ask, receive, rebound, and thrive!

May your new life glorify God and draw others to Him! Amen.

Epilogue

You are a champion; I want you to believe you are and to visualize yourself as one! Champions never quit, no matter how many times they get knocked down or fail. I want you to fight, because God has already given you the weapons for your warfare. Put on those weapons as they are outlined in Ephesians 6:14–18—be truthful, live a holy life, share Christ's good news with others, believe completely in God, confess openly that Jesus Christ is Lord over all, study the Bible frequently, pray often, stay alert, and be patient.

I want you to inspire others by your never-say-die attitude and by your refusal to go away quietly. And when your full deliverance and victory is obtained, do not listen to the devil as he tries to remind you about the past. If God does not condemn you, who else can?

Nobody!

> There is therefore now no condemnation to them which are in Christ Jesus, who walk not after the flesh, but after the Spirit. (Romans 8:1 KJV)

Let the past be the past; do not revisit that life anymore. God promises no more condemnation, but there is a proviso attached to this promise: you must not walk after the flesh, meaning that you must not go back to those things which you have repented of.

It is time to move on. Reject any guilty feelings, and walk tall in your newfound life!

Jesus has promised that when you acknowledge Him as Lord and Savior, you belong to Him and no one can harm you:

> My sheep hear my voice, and I know them, and they follow me: And I give unto them eternal life; and they shall never perish, neither shall any man pluck them out of my hand. My Father, which gave them me, is greater than all; and no man is able to pluck them out of my Father's hand. (John 10:27–29 KJV)

What a promise; what an assurance from the King of Kings and the Prince of Peace. What a declaration from the one who defeated the devil in his own backyard and who is the sole custodian of the keys to hell and death. What a comfort from the one who delivers, restores, and multiplies, continually pleads on our behalf and whose love is more than enough!

God loves you. He has always loved you. And He will always love you. His love is so strong and powerful that He sent Jesus to die on the cross for you. He did this when you did not even know Him. How then can He leave you now?

Impossible!

God never left you, and He will never leave you. Believe again, arise, shine, and soar above every challenge!

Glossary

Champion: Someone who never gives up until he or she is victorious. People with the resolve to keep getting back into line, regardless of the number of setbacks they experience. Champions never quit; they stick around, and oftentimes, victory comes to those who stick with things long enough.

Christ-Led Rebound: The process of recovery from personal challenges, which incorporates biblical instructions, insight, encouragement, and prayers offered to God through His Son, Jesus Christ. It means the complete dependence on the promises of Jesus Christ—that He will set us permanently and completely free when we profess His lordship and obey foundational Christian tenets and commands.

Depression: This can be described as the state of feeling sad, dejected, and hopeless. It is often characterized by inactivity, difficulty in thinking or concentrating, or suicidal tendencies.

Divine Joy: A state of happiness that stems from knowing that God is with you despite your current situation. You ask for this in prayer, as it does not depend on external possessions or well-being but on a person's internal state of mind and attitude. Joy is a gift from God, and with it comes strength to endure challenges.

Faith in Jesus's Name: Believing in the name of Jesus and understanding and leveraging the fact that anything we ask God in the name of Jesus, believing, will be granted us.

Gifts from God: God freely gives His gifts to His children, including mercy, grace, and forgiveness. We do not deserve any good thing from Him due to our sins, but as sovereign King, He decides to bless us anyway due to the sacrifice of Jesus on the cross. Life, health, and prosperity are other examples of God's gifts to His children.

Healing: A reversal of fortunes for the better; this can occur physically (our bodies, circumstances, finances) or emotionally (our mental state). Once God begins the healing process, we are to keep believing and confessing positively.

Internalizing God's Promises: This involves reading the Bible, identifying and thinking on God's promises therein, and making them personal to ourselves. We utilize His promises to fight the devil, wait for our blessings, and stand.

Irrevocable: This is something that cannot be reversed or taken back. God's blessings, gifts, mercies, and forgiveness to us are irrevocable; they are permanent, and we should not therefore let any anxiety come into our thoughts once God has intervened.

Oppression: This can happen if we are under the thumb of the devil. It can be characterized by fearfulness, subdued mind-sets, pessimism, moroseness, and spiritual or mental heaviness. Oppressed people can sometimes be delusional, irrational, and temperamental and apportion blame to others for their inadequacies. They can also suffer nightmares and spiritual attacks, and confuse reality with figments of their imaginations.

Possession: This can happen if someone becomes subservient to the devil, ceding control so the devil uses him or her for his purposes. It could result in the tendency to become a stumbling block for others' relationships with God and with other people.

Power in God's Word: The understanding that God's word created the heavens, the earth, and every living thing. It is knowing what the word (the Bible) says for every situation and claiming those promises for ourselves and knowing that the word of God cannot return without accomplishing what it was sent to do, and standing in firm belief that the Word applies to us too. You have to accept Jesus as Lord and Savior before you can leverage God's word for your benefit; Jesus is the Word of God!

Praise and Worship: Praise involves extolling God for the things He has done for us, or in other cases, for the things we believe He will yet do for us. God can be praised through our voices or by utilizing musical instruments. On the other hand, worship is a higher form of praise; here we extol God for who He is and not necessarily for the things He has done for us. During worship, a person just wants to be in His presence and does not necessarily seek His intervention in a situation; this does not mean that requests cannot be made during worship.

Repression: Feelings of self-denial of God's faithfulness; mental and emotional doubts about God's control over one's affairs. Bottling up of or ignoring the existence of unpalatable thoughts and memories as a self-defense mechanism.

Rest: Complete faith in God. This is a place in our minds where we can relinquish every worry or anxiety and believe without any doubt that God will intervene for our good. It is also the place where the peace of God that passes all understanding is experienced and enjoyed.

Restoration: Receiving back everything we lost during our afflictions and challenging times. After healing comes restoration, and because God is perfect and merciful, He gives us back what we lost and goes further to multiply so we are better off than we were before our afflictions began.

Resurrection: God's capacity to bring life to that which was dead. Knowing God's resurrection power, we are not to give up hope, even when it seems it is too late to remedy our situation. God is never late and will intervene in His own time; our responsibility is to keep on praying and believing despite what we can see in the physical realm.

Sovereignty: The reality that God is King over all things and will therefore be merciful, bountiful, and protective to whomsoever He wishes. A king does not take permission from anyone to bestow his favors to his subjects.

Spiritual Intervention: This is what Jesus does for us in heaven, continually reminding our Father that His death, the cross, and His blood are atoning for our sins, protecting us from judgment, and giving us new beginnings. Anyone who accepts that Jesus also died for him or her receives spiritual intervention and has a high-priestly advocate before God.

Valuing God: This hinges on the fact that God sees, knows, and understands all our actions and the motives behind them. We are therefore to follow His instructions if we truly value Him or acknowledge Him as our heavenly Father. To value God, we have to obey Him.

Yoke: Any challenge we face that might have emanated from the spiritual. Depressions and oppressions are examples of yokes that spring from the devil. Jesus's yoke, however, is easy because He loves us, died for us, and ever lives to intercede for us in God the Father's presence. We are commanded to put on Jesus's yoke.

About the Author

 Dr. Kene D. Ewulu is a professor of organizational leadership and project management, an ordained pastor, and author of the *Christ-Led Rebound Series*. He combines his academic pursuits with an empathetic heart for others, burning with the passion to enable men and women to embrace their mandates as spiritual leaders and moral compasses at home, at work, and in their communities.

Kene is the founder and vice president of the Caleb Assembly, a nonprofit Christian ministry based in Columbia, South Carolina. The Caleb Assembly facilitates seminars and retreats for churches, motivates people in halfway homes, and challenges others to rebound onto righteous living through her global newsletters.

He resides in Columbia with his wife, Ijeoma, and their three teenage children.

Contact

www.thecalebassembly.org

kdewulu@thecalebassembly.org

Other Publications

- *Christ-Led Rebound Principles: Sustaining Christian Deliverance and Victory*

  From: www.amazon.com and www. barnesandnoble.com

- *Christ-Led Rebound Series: Inactivity*
- *Christ-Led Rebound Series: Bad Habits*

  From: www.ReboundSeries.com

Printed in the United States
By Bookmasters